Being a mom is...

By Katherine Brown

Copyright © 2021 Katherine H. Brown

ISBN: 978-1-7367183-3-9

All rights reserved. No part of this publication may be reproduced, stored or transmitted in any form or by any means, electronic, mechanical, photocopying, recording, scanning, or otherwise without written permission from the publisher. It is illegal to copy this book, post it to a website, or distribute it by any other means without permission.

Being a mom is being prepared for every natural disaster on earth at any moment but forgetting to put the milk in the diaper bag for an outing.

Being a mom is sometimes pre-chewing their food just a little because you fear choking.

Being a mom comes with your own perfume... eau de spit up.

Being a mom is always being the least clean family member.

Being a mom is peeing with a tiny audience.

Being a mom is belting out *Old MacDonald Had a Farm* at the drop of a hat or first sign of a cry.

Being a mom is knowing you have the smartest most beautiful tiny human on the planet.

Being a mom is never owning a shirt with an unstretched neckline again.

Being a mom is vowing to keep a strict schedule and watching your tiny human laugh in your face.

Being a mom is having a to-do list of 37 items (including pee alone) with a 45-minute nap window to accomplish them all.

Being a mom is multitasking like a madwoman until one day you find yourself spinning in circles and wondering where you were going (or if it is a really bad day, where your tiny human is).

Being a mom is welcoming insomnia into your life.

Being a mom is being obsessed with watching your tiny human sleep.

Being a mom is being in complete awe that you survived bringing a tiny human into the world.

Being a mom is crying because you can't get any sleep and then crying because your tiny human is spending the night at grandparents' house for the first time.

Being a mom is learning to do everything with only one free hand.

Being a mom is celebrating poopy diapers.

Being a mom is being elated and sad simultaneously every time a developmental milestone occurs.

Being a mom is thanking your parents for not giving you up for adoption on those really hard, cranky days.

Being a mom is equivalent to holding a sign that says please tell me everything you think I'm doing wrong.

Being a mom is owning a whole new level of guilt.... the mom guilt.... over everything.

Being a mom is losing yourself.

Being a mom is finding whole new parts of you.

Being a mom is discovering daily how many of your worst traits your tiny human has.

Being a mom is learning to enjoy cold food.

Being a mom is becoming an interpreter.

Being a mom is driving around nowhere for hours so that your tiny human will sleep.

Being a mom is wearing the same stretchy pants three or four days in a row.

Being a mom is craving adult conversation and then finding yourself unable to talk about anything but your tiny human.

Being a mom is forgetting you can stop swaying and rocking when standing alone.

Being a mom is being a human pillow.

Being a mom is becoming a cuddle addict.

Being a mom is relishing all the tiny human slobber kisses on the cheek as if they were made of gold.

Being a mom is spit up in your belly button.

Being a mom is making eight meals
a day and none are for you.

Being a mom is constantly repeating oneself.

Being a mom is constantly repeating oneself. Oh, sorry, did I already mention that?

Being a mom is becoming reacquainted with every children's song from your childhood.

Being a mom is making up new verses to every nursery rhyme known to man at two in the morning.

Being a mom is...stop me if I've said this before...insomnia.

Being a mom is counting the minutes until nap time.

Being a mom is somehow getting nothing done at nap time.

Being a mom is threatening to throat punch anyone who mentions baby sleep or the lack thereof.

Being a mom is trying to figure out which toy is still making noise.

Being a mom is learning to move with the quietness of a ninja.

Being a mom is becoming adept at picking up a room full toys in less than six minutes.

Being a mom is giving your kid five toys only to have them cry for your water bottle.

Being a mom is begging for your tiny human to sleep in their crib without crying.

Being a mom is dying a little inside when the tiny human does actually start sleeping in their crib.

Being a mom is checking to see if your tiny human is breathing enough times to make your husband consider checking you into a psych ward.

Being a mom is realizing your tiny human must be a diabolical genius who reverse engineered the baby monitor to alert them fifteen minutes after you fall asleep so they can start crying right away.

Every. Time. You. Fall. Asleep.

Being a mom is praying unceasingly for your tiny human to be healthy and safe.

Being a mom is loving so hard it is terrifying.

Being a mom is cursing pajamas made with all snaps as your tiny human learns to practice alligator death rolls.

Being a mom is continuing to lie to yourself that the next stage will be easier.

Being a mom is staring blankly at the next stage as it mocks you with brand new challenges.

Being a mom is never eating ice cream before it melts again.

Being a mom is getting up to eat in the middle of the night your entire pregnancy then being astounded your eight-month-old still always wants to eat at midnight.

Being a mom is taking 7,512 pictures in the first year.

Being a mom is picking someone else's nose willingly.

Being a mom is contending with someone else's poop being on you.

Being a mom is buying yourself things as a reward for keeping your tiny human alive successfully.

Being a mom is stepping on all the toys. All the time.

Being a mom is kicking yourself for not writing down the first time they smiled.

Being a mom is a learning process.

Being a mom is memorizing multiple books so that you can read them to your tiny human with your eyes closed.

Being a mom is the best

.

www.ingramcontent.com/pod-product-compliance
Lightning Source LLC
Chambersburg PA
CBHW072151200426
43209CB00052B/1115